The Grace of God:
Righteousness for Your Situation

By Jeanetta Yeboah

The Grace of God: Righteousness for Your Situation

In Memory of my grandmother, Carrie Lee Mcknight.

Jeanetta Yeboah

Unless otherwise indicated, all scriptures are taken from King James Version (KJV) and New International Version (NIV).

The Grace of God, (The) Righteousness for your situation

ISBN: 1632270595

Copyright © 2015 by Jeanetta Yeboah

Publisher/Editor: Jeanetta Yeboah

Published by: Jeanetta Yeboah

P.O. Box 6171

Moreno Valley, CA 92554

Printed in the United States of America. All rights reserved under International Copyright Law. Contents and/or cover may not be duplicated in any form without written consent.

Preface

"God is the potter and a gold smith. There's nothing that you have done that he cannot fix and heal for you. God wants to move you into your rightful place, his plan for your life. Despite what you have done. He loves you and wants to see you operate at your full potential."

Many people are walking around at this very moment feeling lost, undone, and unworthy of love. Maybe they feel like no one has ever loved them or that they have done things so horribly wrong that the pain they caused is unforgivable. What they may not realize is that they are worthy of love. They have been loved since the beginning of time. They are still loved today. Today they can be forgiven; today they can find salvation, because today God is ready to forgive.

This book was made to inspire and encourage you. This book will make you search your own heart. What do you believe? Are you walking around every day, trying your best to be a testimony to the world, or are you just walking around? Everyone has a purpose. God created us all different for a reason.

"There is grace for the situation that you are facing or neglecting in your life. I am not discounting your experiences, because they were disappointing, hurtful, and possibly even earth-shattering."

No matter what situation you are coming out of, no matter what your nightmares have when you close your eyes, God's sufficient grace can save you. If you've been looking for a sign, looking for some wisdom, looking for a way out of your continuous misery, let this be your first step. Let today be the day that you start a change.

This change will start with the first page of this book and will continue throughout your walk with Christ. ***Today, your life can begin.***

About the Author

Jeanetta Yeboah is a human just like me and you. She had past experiences that she wasn't proud of. She battled with fear, depression, disappointments, and embedded concepts of religion. Things started to change on the first day that she decided to actively seek the face of the Lord for a personal revelation of who He was in her life. She was able to break free of her state of stagnancy and complacency, and she discovered a world of grace, new passions, new desires, and righteousness through the power of God.

God reached into her very heart and made a change. He broke down the walls that she had built around herself, and he replaced them with unconditional love and unique gifts. She was given the gift of intercessory prayer, praise

&worship. She could now be a testimony of Christ to the world, and place Him above all other ideas and objections.

Every day, she continues to see the rewards of following God that have made themselves manifest in her life. Through this book, she is proud to invite you to join the path that God has created for you, and to develop your own relationship with Jesus. This woman is a testimony to everyone that she meets, and there is no doubt that she leaves a lasting impression on the hearts of everyone she encounters.

The Grace of God: Righteousness for Your Situation

Table of Contents

Introduction 1

Chapter 1: Walls and Obstacles 4

Chapter 2: Grace and Righteousness for Your Situation 13

Chapter 3: Forgive Yourself... 34

Chapter 4: A Defining Moment 41

Chapter 5: Spiritual Warfare 48

Chapter 6: If you say what God says, you will have what you say!........ 54

Chapter 7: God Loves You 62

Chapter 8: Dealing with Emotions 70

Chapter 9: Receiving a New Purpose... 74

Chapter 10: Breakthrough 86

Bibles References.. 97

Introduction

If you could write a biography on your life, how would it read, and what would it sound like? Would it be someone else's opinion of you, your personal critic of you, or who God declares that you are? This book is designed to be a healing journal to enable you to evolve into the destiny that God has destined for your life.

As you take this journey with me, I encourage you to allow the spirit of God to minister to you and begin to heal hurts and wounds. The information contained in this book is to allow you to take control of your mind, spirit, and body, and to walk in victory. This information applies to every situation. The information in this book is inspired by the word of God and should not be used as a substitute for the Bible, but it should be used as a word of encouragement. It's not a one-time declaration, but you must remember that declarations/confessions and faith are a part of everyday life in order to walk in victory. Isaiah 55:1(NIV) declares "Come, all you who are thirsty, come to the waters; and you who have no money, come, buy and eat! Come, buy wine and milk without money and without cost." Water is the Spirit of God/his anointing. In order to get the anointing you have to thirst for it and make an exchange. The anointing is the energy life of God flowing through you. So this day I challenge you to receive what is freely given to you and apply it to your life, and watch it change.

Be blessed

Prayer

Heavenly Father, I ask that you come and manifest your spirit upon the readers of this book. Your word says that with you is the fountain of life; in your light we see light Psalm 36:9 (NIV). Come and open the eyes and the heart of the reader to receive a revelation concerning their life that will minister to them and elevate them to a new level.

In Jesus Name, Amen!

Chapter 1
Walls and Obstacles

The enemy desires to create walls and obstacles to withhold us from living our lives to our full potential and from walking into the destiny that God ordained for the believer. **The enemy creates feelings of condemnation, inadequacy, low self-esteem, worldliness, distractions, and deception.** If we allow these feelings to be processed through our mind and heart, they take root creating hindrances, strong holds, and limitations. **Let us throw off everything that hinders and the sin that so easily entangles, and let us run with perseverance the race marked out for us (Hebrews 12:1 NIV).**

To eliminate these obstacles, we have to confront sin and deception, which prevent us from moving forward. Through this process of meditating on the word of God, faith and patience are all necessities that need to be applied in our personal life. These three components are essential because without them, the enemy will begin to infiltrate into our minds and create obstacles. **For consider him that endured such contradiction of sinners against himself, lest ye be wearied and faint in your minds (Hebrews 12:3 KJV).** The obstacles the enemy creates begin first in the mind and then slither into one's heart to create a manifestation of deception. The enemy will use a simple situation to deceive us as believers.

Let's take a look at this situation:

You have been on your job for 10 years; the

economy is effecting most major businesses, so a lot of organizations are beginning to downsize. You have a company meeting in which you learn that downsizing in your organization is going take place before the end of the quarter. Immediately, the enemy will allow your heart to be fearful and begin to tell you that everything that you have worked so hard for will come to an end. Your house will go into foreclosure, your car will be repossessed, and so on. This is one of the tactics of the enemy to play with one's mind. Immediately, you must proceed by rebuking those feelings and declaring that God is your source, and that he is your shield and no good thing will he withhold from you (Psalm 84:11 NIV). What are you doing? You are standing in faith, knowing that God is your source and will provide! So what if it does happen? What if you were one of the individuals that happened to be let go? Do you go into a depression? No! "Call unto me and I will show you great and mighty things that you knoweth not" (Jeremiah 33:3 KJV). By staying in the presence of the Lord, he will direct your steps into your next place of employment. The Lord will seek your prosperity (Psalm 122:9 NIV). This was an actual real life situation and instead of losing a job due to downsizing, this person was asked to run an office in Texas. Look at the grace of God.

Because you are the salt of the earth and God's beloved child, the enemy will try to throw you off course through deception. Deception is a lie that promotes something not of value. Deception begins in the mind. "As a man thinketh, so is he" (Proverbs 23:7 KJV). What you think in your mind portrays who you really are and think that you are going through. Deception allows you to think that you are a product of your own environment. So if you come from a broken home where your father was not present and your mother struggled to provide for you, or you were a victim of incest or mentally challenged, etc., the enemy will use your past to let you know that there is no hope for your future, and you will walk down the same path that your mother/father did. So you begin to process those thoughts and try to be your own savior by taking your life into your hands and looking for love in all the wrong places to end back up where you started. NO WHERE! Just because your mother/father experienced a certain lifestyle of struggles that has been passed down from generation to generation. It stops with you. The bible says that we are free from the curse of the law (Galatians 3:13). The blessings of the Lord maketh rich and addeth no sorrow (Proverbs 10:22) Today by identifying the situation that has been passed down to you, you can destroy it by faith by declaring the word of God with authority. He who is born of God over cometh the world (1 John 5:4). So overcome every situation presenting itself to you as an obstacle through the power of God and the wisdom of God (1 Corinthians 1:24)

Let's stop there for a minute...the Bible says, "He who findeth a wife, findeth a good thing" (Proverbs 18:22 KJV). As a result of their past, some men/women are holding on to loads of baggage in their spirit, meanwhile some are willing to marry at the first opportunity, without collecting data on that individual to see if they are equally yoked. This leads to the vast epidemic of divorces in this country. Sometimes we have to receive Jesus as our husband/wife first, and allow him to make us whole in every aspect of our life, rather than seeking a relationship and approval from another which leads to more bondage. Lastly, you should ask the Lord to guide you to your spouse. As we learned from Samuel, the outer appearance can be deceiving and what looks good to your human eye, might not be good for you.

Prayer

Father, your word says that out of your mouth flows wisdom and understanding. Thank you for imparting your wisdom and understanding in our lives that we may see clearly. Thank you for removing every stumbling block in the way of our victory that we may not continue to go around the same issues, year after year. But catapult us to a new level in the spirit. Let us not be so easily deceived, but give us discernment that we may know what is of you. Let us lean on the foundation of God, with faith that shall never fail...you!

In Jesus Name, Amen!

Journal

Chapter 2
Grace and Righteousness for Your Situation

There is a grace for your situation that you are facing or neglecting in your life. I am not discounting your experiences, because they were disappointing, hurtful, and possibly even earth-shattering. But what I am saying is that you don't have to remain in that present state of mind that you have been teeter-tottering with. What is this situation that you have built a wall within your spirit limiting your capacity to excel in life?

-Are/were you a rape or incest victim?

-Are/were you a drug addict/alcoholic?

-Are/were you facing an addiction?

-Are/were a victim of an unproductive relationship that ended in pain?

-Are you harboring regrets of mistakes that you made as a parent or child?

-Are you still recovering from what the world calls an economic recession (which resulted in lay-offs, and terminations)?

-Are you harboring regrets of an abortion, miscarriage, or lack of fertility?

-Are you holding on to past hurts, un-forgiveness and bitterness?

Dealing with Deception

You have to begin by dealing with the inner you! That is a major challenge, because the inner you has years of disappointments, rejections and memories that need to be recycled into hope. You must begin to say who God says you are instead of who the world or your past experiences say that you are. Everyone has a past of different variations, but everyone has a situation in life that affects them to some degree. "The thief comes only to: steal, kill and destroy. I came that they may have and enjoy life, and have it in abundance (to the full, until it overflows)" (John 10:10 AMP). The enemy takes your bad behavior to make your mind think that you are the way you behave and not the way Christ made you to be. Your behavior doesn't define who you are in Christ. "As he is, so are we" (1 John 4:17 NASB). You have to know that you are the righteousness of God not because of who you are or what you have done, but because of the wonderful sacrifice of Christ on the cross.

Example #1:

You are a mother of two children, and a

faithful hardworking wife. You thought that life was perfect and couldn't be better, until you found out that your husband was cheating on you. Immediately you are crushed, because you did everything you should have done. You exercised, kept the house clean, had a healthy sex life, and you were submissive, fun, and spontaneous. What happened? The enemy will creep in and say, "Well, maybe you aren't pretty enough; you are a size 8 and you should be a size 7. Maybe you aren't good enough." Well, stop right there! The enemy will infiltrate deception into condemnation and inadequacy. This is the point that the enemy will come in and devour your self- worth and make you a victim of your own circumstances. I know that's harsh, but wait—what you went through was horrible. How can a man cheat on a perfect wife and destroy his home? That's horrible, but let's get out of that victim mentality and walk into the enabling power of God that wants to be present in your life. Could there be hope despite the pain? Absolutely. At this point, you would continue to go about life and get God's plan for your future through praying, mediating on his word and listening to the words of the Holy Spirit. The Bible does give you permission to leave your husband in this case. However, I would seek the face of God before making any drastic decisions. God will tell you to go or stay (he's working on that situation). Now if you stay, you must allow the Lord to console you. You have to stay connected during this time, and allow the Lord to begin the healing process. But healing cannot begin without abiding in the word of God. The decision is truly up to you. But remember if God tells you to stay, he has a plan for reconciliation; don't be double-minded (James 1:8). Remember that God is not a man that he should lie, or a son of man that he should change his mind (Numbers 23:19 ESV). Just know that once the Lord speaks, there is a plan for the manifestation of his word, which won't return void.

It's very unfortunate that you had to go through a horrible experience. Many experiences that we go through limit our ability to excel because of past perceptions or encounters that have left a bad memory in our spirits. Also, some experiences we go through get encoded in our DNA. Many people become bitter-numb resulting in their pain being placed on the back burners and their soul silenced while they remain bitter of their experiences. They have an untold message that is silenced because of numbed pain. The numbed pain within their soul has given them the key to survival instead of addressing the problem, and so they walk in medicated bitterness without a solution or cure.

I encourage you to adhere to the one solution that can change your life: the grace of God. In the inner chamber of your soul, you might begin to wonder, *Why did God allow this to happen to me? Why must I endure these years of pain?* Before you begin to get technical and all religious, allow me to explain.

If you can put a book mark right there, let's take a look at (Job Chapter 1:6-12 NIV):

> One day the angels came to present themselves before the Lord, and Satan also came with them. The Lord said to Satan, "Where have you come from?" Satan answered the Lord, "From roaming

throughout the earth, going back and forth on it."

Then the Lord said to Satan, "Have you considered my servant Job? There is no one on earth like him; he is blameless and upright, a man who fears God and shuns evil." "Does Job fear God for nothing?" Satan replied. "Have you not put a hedge around him and his household and everything he has? You have blessed the work of his hands, so that his flocks and herds are spread throughout the land. But now stretch out your hand and strike everything he has, and he will surely curse you to your face." The Lord said to Satan, "Very well, then, everything he has is in your power, but on the man himself do not lay a finger." Then Satan went out from the presence of the Lord.

Through the course of time, that which was very important to Job was taken away, and the very people around began to question his actions. What did he do wrong? It came to a point, where Job began to have an intimate conversation with the Lord during his hurtful time. It was then, the Lord began to give Job an account of his un-limitless, matchless power. Yet his experience was very crucial in the eyes of the modern-day viewpoint. Job stood. HE STOOD. At the end of the journey, he was restored and received twice as much as he had before in Job 42.

I can't explain to you why God allowed you to walk or endure certain situations. But I am here right now to help you understand what he can do for you now. God is getting ready to give you a new heart. "A new heart also will I give you and a new spirit will I put within you; and I will take away the stony heart out of your flesh, and I will give you a heart of flesh" (Ezekiel 36:26). As you receive this word, and allow the word of God to abide in your spirit, you will begin to see a shift in your life. As we have learned from Job, you have to be careful who you allow to speak into your life. Don't worry about what people will say as you begin this walk of grace and renew your mind in the word of God, people will talk. They will have opinions about how truly renewed your mind is, how delivered you are, what you use to do, and if the works of God have truly manifested in your life.

However if what they are saying doesn't match up with the word of God and his grace. They are talking babble and not bible. One incorrect word of someone can destroy your life because it will take you down the path of destruction. I learned this a long time ago. Someone spoke a word of reality to me which was true physically, meanwhile I was speaking the word of God over this situation. It nearly destroyed me and put me in a state of depression because I began to be my own God and fix my situation. Instead of allowing my mind to stay renewed and let God in his own timing, I was listening to man evaluate my situation. As I was lying in bed depressed the lord asked me, does what they say line up with my word? Is that what my word has to say about it. Think on those things which are lovely and pure and cast down every imagination that riseth above the word of God. Instantly my spirit was released from weariness, depression and bondage. Wow a three-minute conversation almost destroyed my life.

So who cares what people thinks or what opinion of your life is. It's not their philosophy or opinion that matters but the word of God flowing inside of your life. The word of God should be a waterfall flowing on ever situation that comes your way. Every situation you have has a solution in the word of God. So who cares what people are saying? They were talking about you from the very beginning. You just happen to find out about it through direct contact or a gossiping individual. Therefore gird yourself up and renew your mind. You can't have the strength of a little child whose always conscious of what people are saying about them or willing to please everyone by listening to everything people say. No, now that you are in Christ you obey the word of God literally. Yes people will laugh but once the power of God hits your life and brings physical manifestation. They won't be laughing.

What Is Grace? Why Do I Need It?

God's grace is unmerited favor towards man. Through his unlimited power, he can do what you can't do you on your own. God's grace empowers you to overcome all shortcomings and downfalls and to walk in your rightful place. Grace enables you to stand on the promises of God and his word. Everyone on this earth has a purpose, yet God has given us all free will. However, it's not his heart's desire that his people neglect their purpose on earth and endure hurtful pain.

"The thief comes only to steal and kill and destroy; I have come that they may have life, and have it to the full" (John 10:10 NIV). The Lord desires that you walk in fullness. When he died upon the cross for us, it wasn't just for our sins.

He has redeemed us so that we can walk in victory. Every struggle or situation has already been nailed to the cross. Stop medicating them.

"Come to me, all you who are weary and burdened, and I will give you rest" (Matthew 11:28 NIV). There's an incredible rest that comes upon us when we rest in his finished works. Our situations have already been nailed to the cross. When we rest in his finished works, we are telling God that we trust him to take care of all of our concerns. Resting in the Lord isn't easy. In fact, the Bible refers to it as labor. "Let us, therefore, make every effort to enter that rest" (Hebrews 4:11 NIV). If we need to enter into his rest, why is it labor and where does grace fit in? It's labor because you are working against your natural human tendencies to make things happen for you and allowing God to work on your behalf. Please be mindful resting is not being idol. Whatever you are believing God to do, as you move forward by the guidance of the Holy Spirit, rest to know that what you can't do, God will do.

Grace and righteousness fit in as we begin to know who we are in Christ. The Bible refers to us as priests of righteousness in (Psalms 132:9 NIV). "God made him who had no sin to be sin for us, so that in him we might become the righteousness of God" (2 Corinthians 5:21 NIV).

Am I insinuating that you are righteous and a recipient of God's grace, despite all that you have been through and done? Yes, I am! Your grace and righteousness is a gift from God himself, however you must desire it. "For many invited, but few are chosen (Matthew 22:14)." The Lord desires all of us to receive what is freely given to us, but unfortunately not everyone has the desire to seek after what is rightfully given to them. What is righteousness? Righteousness is to be made in right standing with God. "This righteousness is given through faith in Jesus Christ to all who believe" (Romans 8:22 NIV). Righteousness allows us to walk into our rightful place with God, because we know who we are and in whom we trust. Therefore, any situations in our lives that brings condemnation, the righteousness that dwells within us rises up to cast it down.

Condemnation is cast down because Romans 8:1 says, "Therefore, there is now no condemnation for those who are in Christ Jesus." Your righteousness is confirmed in (Romans 5:17 NIV), "For if, by the trespass of the one man, death reigned through that one man, how much more will those who receive God's abundant provision of grace and of the gift of righteousness reign in life through the one man, Jesus Christ!" That verse sums it up very well. You are righteous!

Since we have concluded that you are righteous, your life has to change. It is impossible to be righteous and seek after the grace of God (meditating and declaring his word) and your life remain the same. Let me give you some scriptures that talk about grace:

"God is able to make all grace abound upon you (2 Corinthians 9:8 NIV)."

"But to each of us grace has been given as Christ apportioned it (Ephesians 4:7 NIV)."

"Grace and peace be yours in abundance through the knowledge of God and of Jesus our Lord (2 Peter 1:2 NIV)

"We believe it is through the grace of our

Lord Jesus that we are saved (Acts 15:11 NIV)

Your life has to change by the grace of God, as you earnestly desire and seek God for yourself. This was something that I didn't get years ago. I just couldn't believe that receiving Gods grace was so easy. I thought I literally had to fast for 90 days, prayer for hours at a time (avoiding my family) and so on. But you don't. His grace is right in front of you, just grab it right now in your spirit and let God begin to minister to you, guide and direct you.

Prayer

Dear Heavenly Father,

I thank you for the life of the individual that is reading this book. Thank you for your word that says, "No weapon formed against us shall prosper." Thank you that indeed that is the case with the individual that is reading this book. That, despite all that they have been through, the weapon (destruction meant for them) wasn't able to prosper. They survived through the disappointments, hurts, and pain. Thank you, Lord, for your angels encamping around them on this journey, protecting them.

Father, lastly, thank you for your gifts of grace and righteousness that you have given them as your children. That despite all condemnation, nothing can make them unrighteous or remove your grace from them. Father begin to pour your revelation upon this individual reading this book right now. Where ever they are struggling to receive your grace and righteousness upon their life, begin to pour your Holy Spirit upon them to minister unto them.

In Jesus Name, Amen!

Journal

Chapter 3
Forgive Yourself

It's time to forgive yourself. If God himself (who is the ultimate judge) has forgiven you, why do you continually harbor unforgiveness concerning yourself? "For I will forgive their wickedness and will remember their sins no more" (Hebrews 8:12). What have you done that you cannot be forgiven? What bitterness are you holding unto? I met a very wealthy woman who made a bad decision only to end up losing her riches about two months ago. As I began to minister to the lady, she began to talk about how she supported each and every need of her family, until she found herself broke. When she was in need, she only found herself trying to climb back to the top by herself with no help. Wow, how bitter she was, as she began to cry and express her inner hurts numbly.

God is the potter and a gold smith. There's nothing that you have done that he cannot fix and heal you from. God wants to move you into your rightful place and into his plan for your life despite what you have done. He loves you and wants to see you operate at your full potential. Jeremiah 18:6 says, "You are the clay in the potter's hands, and I am the potter." In this text, Jeremiah was the clay and the Lord was the potter. In relation to your life, God will mold and shape your life for the sole purpose of the glory going back to him.

Stop judging and condemning yourself. God has forgiven you. So why are you withholding your own forgiveness when God who has all power to forgive you of your past? The Bible says, "Your sins, he remembers no more."

Many times the forgiveness we withhold from ourselves, we also withhold from others, which in turn bring sickness and disease to our life.

Relationships are often ruined due to unforgiveness and due to emotions and the effects of spiritual warfare in which we aren't trained to battle. Our relationships fail, which is very unfortunate. Many times when we are battling with unforgiveness and fail to forgive because our pain becomes bitter-numb. Bitter numb? Yes, we get so angry, and when the thought of forgiving that person comes across, we become numb (as if we were never upset or angry with that particular individual). Meanwhile, unknowingly our bodies are suffering the consequences of the stress of unforgiveness, which is contributing to it. Am I saying that unforgiveness can cause health problems? Yes, because the body releases certain enzymes and when we get to the state that we are bitter (hurt, sad, depressed) it contributes towards our cholesterol and blood pressure levels rising, which results in headaches, ulcers, heart attacks, panic attacks, asthma, death and the list goes on. Unforgiveness was a topic of interest to Peter in Matthew 18:21. He asked the Lord, "How many times shall I forgive my brother who sins against me? Up to seven times?" Seven times seems very modest. But Jesus took it one step further, he told Peter in verse 22, "I tell you not seven times, but seventy times seven." One key component to forgiveness is love.

In Matthew 22, Jesus says, "Love your neighbor as you love yourself." When you aren't able to walk in love, you are doubting the word of God and doubt is the one thing that hindered the Israelites from entering the Promised Land. It's not an easy thing to forgive or to love your neighbor, but the power of the Holy Spirit will enable us to do, what we can't ordinarily do with our natural human abilities.

Prayer

Father, I commit my brother/sister right now into your hands.

Anywhere in their hearts where they have hidden any form of unforgiveness, I pray for your grace of forgiveness to empower them to love their neighbor. As they forgive, let them walk in the power of your love. May those people in their lives that are hard to interact with on an intermittent interaction or permanent, be able to be loved with grace.

In Jesus Name, Amen!

Journal

Chapter 4
A Defining Moment

A defining moment is when you have learned that you had something of value and never knew it. Many believers have been walking with God and never utilizing the equipment that he has given them to use: grace and righteousness. It's like a mechanic never utilizing the jack to lift the car, but rather instead substituting it with something else. Jesus is the jack that the mechanic failed to realize that he needed to use. Jesus lifts the weight of our situations in life, empowering us to walk in total victory and success.

All these years you have been operating as your own savior with limited success. As believers, we have to constantly remind ourselves who we are in Christ, because the situations we face in life try to challenge our righteousness in Christ and who we are in Christ. Your righteousness is a gift from God. The term *gift* is often taken lightly because gifts range from cheap to expensive. However, every gift that comes from Christ has an expensive price tag on it. What price would you put on him dying on the cross to give you eternal life? That alone is an expensive price tag. Well, so is grace and righteousness. It's not something that can be earned, bribed, bought, exchanged, or duplicated. Neither is grace and righteousness a raffle ticket to go out and sin using them as a scapegoat to cover up your true intentions.

A defining moment in one's life is when they come into contact with the truth. In this case, the truth is Jesus Christ. (John 10:10) "I come that

I may give life and life more abundantly. But when the spirit of truth comes, he will guide you in all truth" (John 16:13 NLT). The truth is you have received the gifts of grace and righteousness and your sins he remembers no more (Psalm 103:1- 3). Once you operate in this defining moment, you can't let "defining people killers" come in and destroy your defining revelation. People are very interesting. Let's just take a look back at Job; the people around him tried to define him by his present situation, as if they themselves were on the throne panel of judgment with God himself. People can't define you by your past, because if the creator himself says, "He remembers your sins no more!" So who are people to judge you because of your past situations that you have experienced in life? They are defining people killers. They don't want you to open up the inner chamber of your soul to receive what God has for you. Rather, they feel that you should remain in a state of complacency because they don't feel that you are ready to receive the gift that God has for you.

Therefore, they challenge you to challenge the creator, as the people around Job did. The gift of grace and righteousness comes automatically once you get saved. Did you notice you didn't have to ask to receive those gifts? No, you didn't. It came upon you when you accepted Jesus Christ as your savior! You just have to activate them in faith.

Question: What happens if I never accept Jesus Christ as my personal savior?

Answer: Then let's do it now!

Repeat after me: *Father, I thank you that you died upon the cross for me, bearing my iniquities,* *sickness, and situations. Not only did you die on the cross, you rose again giving me eternal life. This day, I receive you as my personal Lord and Savior over my life. Come and take control over my life, and live in me. Take out anything that's not of you in my life. Forgive me of my sins. I believe that you died on the cross and on the third day you rose from the dead. Allow me to walk in my rightful purpose. In Jesus' name. Amen.*

You are now saved! Receive your gifts.

Prayer

Father, I thank you for this defining moment for my sister and my brother reading this book. Thank you for removing defining people killers out of their midst, challenging them to challenge your ability to do what you said that you would in their life's. But elevate them to a new level now that they have come into contact with the truth, which is what you have freely given them, grace and righteousness for them to walk in. Let them walk boldly in these gifts despite of every shortcoming and downfall knowing that every situation, addiction, circumstance that they face in their life shall melt away as wax because of your mighty power upon their life. Continue to reveal your grace and righteousness to them in greater detail.

In Jesus Name, Amen!

Jeanetta Yeboah

Journal

Chapter 5
Spiritual Warfare

What is spiritual warfare? Spiritual warfare is an attack on your mind, insinuating that what God said that he was going to do in your life will not come to pass. The enemy, through tactical means, creates certain situations in attempt for you to forsake your faith in the word of God over your life. Going through situations in life, as we saw in the book of Job, is not easy, but as believers every battle/fight we face is a good fight, because we win. "Thanks be unto God who always causeth us to triumph in Christ" (2 Corinthians 2:14 KJV). The ultimate secret to spiritual warfare is in (Ephesians 6:10 AMP) "In conclusion, be strong in the Lord [be empowered through your union with Him]; draw your strength from Him [that strength which His boundless might provides]. Put on God's whole armor [the armor of a heavy-armed soldier which God supplies], that you may be able to successfully to stand up against [all] the strategies *and* the deceits of the devil. For we are not wrestling with flesh and blood [contending only with physical opponents], but against the despotisms, against the powers, against [the master spirits who are] the world rulers of this present darkness, against the spirit forces of wickedness in the heavenly (supernatural) sphere." This verse is very crucial because your success lies within the obedience of this verse. To put on the whole armor of God means to study the word of God. Saturating the word of God in our life.

We have to rest and know that we can't self-medicate ourselves with our self-effort. We must labor to enter the rest of God through the word of God, in which we are able to pull down strongholds. A stronghold is a form of captivity that takes place in your mind and is meant for you to think contrary to the word of God. "For the weapons of our warfare are not carnal, but mighty through God to the pulling down of strongholds" (2 Corinthians 10:4). During spiritual warfare, when strongholds and spiritual wickedness arise, we have to enter in knowing that the battle has already been won. Christ has given you the tools to succeed: his word, faith, and your mouth. Now you must put it to work by working from victory that Jesus won for you on the cross, into physical manifestation. For he has already paid the price. Your victory lies in your faith. "For everyone born of God overcomes the world. This is the victory that has overcome the world, even our faith" (1John 5:4).

Please note, this isn't just a confession but a belief that rises out of you in time of difficulties with assurance in the promises of God. The true character of someone comes out in times of stress, and difficulties; it is then and there that you see what they really believe. Psalm 46:1-3, 5: "God is our refuge and strength, an ever- present help in times of trouble. Therefore, we will not fear, though the earth give way and the mountains fall into the heart of the sea, though its waters roar and foam and the mountains quake with their surging." There is assurance in this verse that God is your refuge and whatever situation you are facing right now in life has an expiration date. This too shall pass. Don't fear, stand strong on the word of God.

Prayer

Father, thank you for this brother/sister that's engaging in this prayer with you now. Thank you that you are their source and strength. Thank you for a sound mind and clarity in this season for them. That despite what is going on around them or in their life, they will still hold on to their faith and confession in your word with assurance, knowing that the victory has already been won. Thank you that the situation that they are going through is already a fixed fight. They have won, because you already paid the price by overcoming the world. Continue to lead and guide them through this journey that will give you all the glory.

In Jesus Name, Amen!

Jeanetta Yeboah

Journal

Chapter 6
If you say what God says, you will have what you say!

Too often as Christians we operate by our five senses. We always say how we feel, what we see, and don't have. But as Christians, we should be operating in a greater anointing and saying that what we don't have is on its way. But out of fear and shame, we limit our blessings based upon what people would think of us. We should be professing: *I am healed, my child is delivered; it is well.* Too often, we see blessings on a tangible outlook of what God is doing. God is not a tangible God. He creates things in the spirit, and then it's manifested. That's why the scriptures say, "Though the waters roar." Things will get loud, distracting, and chaotic to you. But you have to make a decision to stand upon your righteousness God has given you and confess what the word of God says about you in confidence. God has given you divine authority in your mouth. There is power in your tongue.

The Bible says life and death is in the power of your tongue (Proverbs 18:21). In Matthew 11:12, it states that the kingdom of heaven suffereth violence and the violent take it by force. What I am saying here is that you have a purpose—everyone has a purpose on this earth. Yes, I know life has dealt you some situations that were uncomfortable for you. If you're not dead God, still has a purpose to be fulfilled in your life. He has brought you through that to another level and life. The Bible says that many are the afflictions of the righteous but the Lord delivers him from them all (Psalm 34:19).

What dead situation do you have in your life? What dream has been left abandoned without a glimpse of hope? Be like Ezekiel. In Ezekiel chapter 37, you see the Lord ask Ezekiel a very interesting question. In verse 3, he states, "Can these dry bones live?" Then in verse 7, the Lord commands Ezekiel to prophesy to the dry bones, and the Bible says that "suddenly" there was a noise and rattling. Suddenly, there was a noise! Wow. What was happening here? He opened his mouth. Open your mouth concerning every situation that is dormant, dead, or out of order in your life. Use the authority to speak over the situations, because there is power in your mouth. So speak!

However, please don't abuse your power, because your time will be in vain. What do I mean? Well, if you see a married man/woman, and your mind is telling you that he/she is your husband/wife, you can't use your mouth to command their husband/wife to die, so that you can be their new spouse. That's called insanity and witchcraft, which is powerless compared to the matchless power of Jesus Christ. My second point is speaking careless things into your life. Things like, "good things never happen to me, I will never get married, I am so sick!" What are you doing? You are speaking into atmosphere words that are circling around looking for a place to manifest. "For as he thinks in his heart, so is he" (Proverbs 23:7). After repeatedly speaking meaningless things over your life, you will begin to think them, causing them to manifest, unless you begin to change the way you think.

In order to get what God says in your life,

you have to know his word. When you get your thinking in line with the word of God, it becomes a parallel witness to your spirit. In other-words, your spirit becomes a witness to the living word of God in your life. As you spend time in his word, meditating upon his promises, you will ultimately stumble into a *Rhema* word for your situation. A simple definition of a *Rhema* word is a fresh word for your situation, beyond the natural inclination of man. Through spending time in the word of God, you will stumble across scriptures such as (John 15:7 KJV), "If ye abide in Me, and My words abide in you, ye shall ask what ye will, and it shall be done unto you. This scripture is affirming what Joshua 1:8 says by declaring, meditate upon the word of God. When you meditate upon the word of God, it is abiding in you! Therefore, you can ask the Lord for the desires in your heart. To take it one step further, if your desires aren't good, the Lord will plant his desires in your heart (now becoming one with your desires found in Psalm 37:4). It becomes a natural impartation for the Holy Spirit into your spirit. Once your desires are formed, you begin your declaration process of speaking the word of God. Then watch it come to pass.

Prayer

Father, thank you for my sister/brother who are reading this and joining me in prayer. Thank you for the authority you have given them to speak life over their life that can change any situation through your word. Thank you for inward transformation in the way that they think and talk. That they will begin to think the thoughts that you think towards them. To get a wider view point of who you called them to be. Thank you for a turnaround in their life and letting them see the blessings of speaking your word over their life.

In Jesus Name, Amen!

Jeanetta Yeboah

Journal

Chapter 7
God Loves You

God loves you. Despite what has happened in your life, God has a plan for your life and he wants you to embrace his presence, power and love, to walk in victory. Now you are at a cross road. Do you **a)** stop being a victim, and walk into God's presence full of love and peace; or **b)** remain the victim and hold on to resentment, bitterness and anger?

Walking in God's love and peace will mandate that you rely on his grace. Grace is God's enabling power to do something that you can't do on your own. You can't love someone that hurt you without relying on the love and grace of God to work through you. You can't pick up the pieces from a failure without grasping God's love and grace for your life. "My grace is sufficient for you, for my power is made perfect in weakness" (2 Corinthians 12:9). Well, how do you go about receiving God's grace through natural works (Romans 11:6)? No, you obtain grace through faith!

It seems like it should be so much more to grace than receiving it through faith. It just seems so easy, yet it is so hard for many believers to do, because they feel that they have to physically contribute towards the final decision of their situation. When we begin to take situations in our own hands, it reflects how we feel inwardly towards the power of God despite the religious mask that we wear on the outside. It reflects fear and doubt because we don't know if God is going to work the problem out the way that we are expecting. But how many of you know that every outcome/path that the Lord creates for us is good (1Timothy 4:4)?

Relying on the Lord's wisdom and grace doesn't mean that the enemy is not going to come against you...because his plan is to get you off track. But you have to prepare yourself mentally that you have the victory and it has already came to pass. You are just waiting on the physical manifestation from the spiritual realm. You have to be able to speak back to situations when your mind is presenting adverse thoughts like: *Haven't you been in this situation for nine years? What makes you think that it's going to change?* You have to be able to come back and say this situation will change because greater is he that is in me than he that is in the world (1 John 4:4). Since you are born of God, you overcome the afflictions the world attempts to bring against you, because you are victorious (1John 5:4).

Example #1

You go for a doctor's checkup because of some complications you have been experiencing. After running several tests, it comes back that you have cancer. Immediately, the enemy will began to tell you that you are going to die, your children will be left without a mother/father, and all your goals will go unfulfilled. No, you begin to declare that you shall live and not die (Psalm 118:17); by his stripes you are healed (Isaiah 53:5). You begin to declare to spectators that the doctor's report states that you have cancer, but your father's report declares that you can't have cancer and that you are healed, because God's blood isn't tainted.

Let's take a look at another example #2:

I know an incredible woman (very dear to

my heart) who received a report from the doctor that she needed a blood transfusion. This transfusion was high risk for her because she had so many health conditions, and the risk of being on Coumadin could cause unnecessary problems for her. At this particular point she was already in the hospital for an existing situation and she had no choice but to consent to the blood transfusion so that the doctors could finish her procedure she was originally admitted for. As they were reviewing with her the cons of the blood transfusion, they advised her that it was a 50/50 chance that she could live. Immediately, she looked at me, as I was in the room with a look of peace on my face. I declared that she was covered by the blood of Jesus and that the blood transfusion would be intertwined with the blood of the lamb. Let me tell you, today she is alive and living. Glory be to God. The difference is in your declarations and your thoughts, because the power is in your tongue (Proverbs 18:21).

Prayer

Father, thank you for your grace upon the reader of this book. Thank you for allowing them to seek your grace like never before. Thank you for your unconditional love, that shall never cease. Thank you for them bumping into grace in every situation in their lifes. Thank you for your grace over their: children, marriage, finances, career, health, destiny. Thank you Lord that you were rich but became poor that they can become abundantly supplied in every area of their life. As they grasp this grace Lord, let them become a testimony that leads others to you.

In Jesus Name, Amen!

Jeanetta Yeboah

Journal

Chapter 8
Dealing with Emotions

Love is unconditional but it doesn't always feel good to love. Therefore, we walk by the Spirit of God so when he tells us to walk in love, we must deny our five senses and begin to walk by the Spirit.

There is a familiar text in the Bible where Jesus said, "As you have done to them you have done unto me." You never know who God is calling you to love, but whoever God is calling you to love, they might not be easy to love, but you're planting a seed of unconditional love.

Many of our five senses have created havoc in our lives because our emotions are out of whack. When you play in the flesh, you limit

God's ability and supernatural power to perform mighty works in your life. When you walk in the flesh, you're saying that the ultimate beauty of what God's word says it's not important in your life—what's important is your five senses, but the last time I checked my Bible, it said, "Acknowledge me in all of your ways, and I shall direct your path (Proverbs 3:6)"

Prayer

Father, thank you for the love that you continually express concerning my brother/sister. Thank you that through your righteousness, they are righteous; because they are righteous they have a right to receive the blessings that you have proclaimed in your word. Thank you for grace for every uncomfortable situation that you have called them to be in. That the light that you have placed in them will shine. Thank you for allowing them to walk away from their five senses and begin to see things as you see them. Thank you for the anointing of ease, and carrying the burden for my brother/sister as they surrender unto you.

In Jesus Name, Amen!

Jeanetta Yeboah

Journal

Chapter 9
Receiving a New Purpose

What is the deepest desire of your heart? Delight yourself in the Lord and he will give you the desires of your heart (Psalm 37:4). And secret petitions of your heart. As you do this, he places desires within you.

This a very profound scripture because it says what God will do for us because after being in the presence of the Lord, he will drop desires that came from him to make them your desires. I say his desires because he imparted them in your spirit to make you passionate about a certain thing.

This applies to every area of your life from relationships, emotions, recovering from setbacks, future plans, and much more... A simple impartation from the Lord can give one a fresh new start on life.

Let's take a look at an example #1:

A 10-year-old girl living in an abusive family environment in the projects finds herself abruptly taken from her family to enter foster care in which the tradition of abuse followed her from foster home to foster home. At the age of 18, she had an encounter with the Lord that changed her life. Instantly without notice, 17 years of hurt and flashbacks of agony became a healing zone and inspiration for her to start her own non- profit organization for disadvantaged children. As wounded as she was, she had lost all hope and the Lord gave her a desire that would change the inner cities of every state. Despite her conflicted childhood full of hurt and disappointments, she still allowed the Lord into her life. After all, He kept her through all the abuse, neglect, incest and hurt.

Let's take a look at another example #2:

A rising entrepreneur and bachelor working in his barbershop was struggling to make ends meet, but had a desire to open a culinary business. Thirsty for success but limited by financial resources, he was ready to challenge God on his promises. Ready to see if God is really who He says He is, he begins to meditate on Psalm 37. Then he stumbles upon Deuteronomy 28:5:"Blessed shall be your basket and your kneading bowl." Instantly, the Lord dropped in his spirit the understanding of this scripture. That whatever brought wealth in his basket and to his kneading bowl shall be blessed. Immediately, he received the word in his spirit but began to size the revelation from the Lord up; until he heard Deuteronomy 8:18. "The Lord give thee power to get wealth."Not too long afterwards, he noticed himself mediating on these scriptures and he had a divine encounter with the Lord while cutting his client's hair. Prior to opening his own barber shop, he was a chef by trade, but due to financial difficulties, he had to go where the money was and put his culinary dream on the back burner. The Lord gave him a desire to start making unique pastries to sell to clients and to start doing catering on the weekends. This was a divine encounter from the Lord. He put his culinary desire on the back burner and the Lord revived it. Not before long, the Lord caused his culinary business to expand so much that he had to open a facility and start hiring people. How did this happen? The Lord gave him those desires. So what do you think? You might be thinking, well, that was him, but what about me?

We are in covenant with God. Confessions and declarations don't just happen in prayer, but it's a part of our daily faith walk with God. I'm not saying these individuals never experienced a difficult time but they persevered through the difficulties and spiritual warfare and walked into their blessings...their wealthy place. After experiencing a non-productive life or a life of disappointments, how do I get to the place where I can hear the voice of the Lord clearly? That's simple—the Bible says that his sheep know his voice (John 10:27). You get to know his voice by spending time with him in the spirit.

Example #3

In 1 Samuel 16, the Lord is speaking to Samuel about a specific task he has given him to anoint the new king in which he predestined. However, Samuel was caught in his emotions mourning for someone who the Lord had demoted, but in verse 4, we see Samuel setting out on his task (out of obedience). Many times in life, God will give us a task in which we have to literally take each direction through the voice of the Holy Spirit. When Samuel arrived at his destination, the Lord advised Samuel not to look at the outer appearance, because the Lord looks at the heart. The Lord knew that Samuel would pick the new king out of his personal preference; therefore, the Lord guided him through the selection of all the sons of Jesse. Through the guidance of the Holy Spirit, David the least likely son (by appearance who tended to the sheep) was selected to be king by the Lord himself, who then became one of the greatest kings.

Examples #4

Everyone knows the familiar story of Moses (who had a speech impediment), and how God used him to deliver 600,000 Israelites out of Egypt in the middle of the night. As they were leaving, Pharaoh had a change of heart, and Pharaoh sent 600 of his best chariots in attempt to enslave them again. But the Lord had a different plan. As they looked back, they saw their enemies coming (the people began to fear), and immediately the Lord gave him a divine direction. He said in verse 21 of Exodus Chapter 14, the Lord dried out the Red Sea. Through his obedience, the people of Israel were delivered immediately at the blink of an eye.

Example #5

Matthew 1:20 says, "Joseph son of David, do not be afraid to take Mary home as your wife, because what is conceived in her is from the Holy

Spirit." What was going on here? Filled, with emotions, Joseph was planning to secretly send Mary away. But the Lord knew his plans, and therefore sent his angel to minister to Joseph in a dream. Yes, in a dream. There are many ways that the Lord speaks to us, you can't put the Lord in a box, because he can't fit in your small box.

These examples are meant to encourage you, knowing that listening to the voice of the Lord is a rewarding experience. This experience can be used in your life to experience great victories in your life or simply watch the power of God move in someone's life. Which is exactly what happened to me. Several years ago, as I beginning to grasp the message of grace, I was attending prayer at church praying for my needs. As I was in prayer the Lord told me that he wanted to me to be a prayer intercessor for his people (the pastor, the world and the needs of the people). That as I prayed for his people, he would work in every area of my life. I was shocked because I had issues that needed to be addressed like yesterday, I thought all my attention should go towards that? The whole week the Lord pressed a heavy burden in my heart to pray for his people, that wouldn't leave. What was happening here? The Lord was changing my desires. So when prayer resumed at church, I had already in my spirit accepted the assignment of God. Only to be confronted by the church to be on the prayer team. God was working behind the scenes, and worked everything out. As we began to pray, people who were barren became pregnant, people with court cases received victory, people who were sick became healed, and it was for the glory of God. Simultaneously, situations in my life that seemed impossible, began to crumble right before my face. "Seek first his kingdom and his righteousness, and all these things shall be added to you (Matthew 6:33 NIV)." So this principle has changed my life from that very point, still today I am focused on the uplifting of God's kingdom. So before you get caught up with everything that's going on in your life, remember to focus on Gods kingdom.

Operate in the anointing God has given you to be a servant in his kingdom. Don't get caught up in positions and titles. But humble yourself by being a good steward for Christ in the kingdom of God.

Prayer

Father, thank you for that paradigm shift for my brother and sister in this season. Even as they have declared your word over their life, they are beginning to walk in the boldness of their authority you have given them. Thank you for your voice in this season. As you guide and lead them, they will walk into their place of abundance and prosperity in every area concerning their life. As they are walking in this new season, thank you for that divine encounter with you that changes their focal point of their lives into victory. Amen.

Jeanetta Yeboah

Journal

Chapter 10
Breakthrough

I declare out of my mouth a season of change for you! God is about to work out the intimate details of your life to give you healing, restoration, peace, and victory in every area of your life. When fear tries to creep in and say the opposite of what God says, begin to reflect on the promises of God concerning your situation. Begin to praise God and expect to see physical manifestation. If you say what God says, then you will have what you say. God inhabits the praises of his people (Psalm 22:3). As Jehoshaphat was facing an impossible situation, notice the strategy that he underwent: they began to praise the Lord. As they began to praise, the Lord set up ambushes against his enemies and immediately the victory was won.

You have already been given the victory, so why do you worry and doubt about the outcome of what God said that he would do? Surrender your total trust to him, and set your eyes like flint to see the victory. Don't look at the residue because it is a mirage that is intended to distract you and take you off course. Don't worry about the outstanding situations in your life. Your past mistakes don't dictate your future once we are in Christ. Just know that the victory is yours.

A familiar text in the Bible is John 6:21. The verses leading up to it refer to the disciples going into a boat without Jesus only to encounter a great wind and the sight of Jesus walking on water. The point I want to focus on is when they were willing to let Jesus on their boat. The Bible says that "immediately" they were on the other side, referring to their destination. In this season as you allow Jesus in your: boat, life, business, situation (whatever it may be), you will experience life-changing results! Why? When you allow Jesus to come, you have to totally surrender and relinquish all fears.

Surrendering and relinquishing fears is exactly what we saw in 1 Kings 17, which created "an immediate situation." We saw:

1. Elijah received divine directions from God to receive food and water by going to the brook.
2. We also saw the Zarephath woman who was declaring death over her life, experience an immediate change upon her obedience. As a result, she experienced a harvest and her

declarations of death were reversed. That life-changing situation can happen in your life as well.

The Bible declares, "For as long as there the earth endures, seedtime and harvest, cold and heat, summer and winter, day and night will never cease" (Genesis 8:22). The Zarephath woman out of her obedience to sow a seed into the man of God's life, experienced a harvest. Why? Because of the principle of sowing and reaping. Buts it's important that your seed falls on good ground, and that you water it with the word of God and faith. What is good ground? "Still other seed fell on good soil, where it produced a crop--a hundred, sixty or thirty times what was sown" (Matthew 13:8). Once you sow your seed, you then wrap your need around the seed of what you are believing God to do in your life, casting away all doubt. I encourage you to sow a $58.00 victory seed to your church, which is symbolic of the 58 types of blessings in the Bible. But wherever you decide to sow, make sure that you sow on good ground, which is a church grounded on the word of God.

As you sow this seed, wrap your need around that seed. As you are believing God for your need, God is also doing other things in your life. Sowing doesn't just produce financial harvest but also peace, joy, healing, restoration and much more. A lady was in need of a drastic breakthrough in her life. She sowed a seed wrapping her need around that seed only to find herself the next day admitted into the hospital with a swollen leg and unable to walk. As she called me, I encouraged her to water that seed she sowed. Two days later, after running several tests in the hospital, the doctors couldn't find anything wrong with her. Why? The Lord had healed her. She planted a seed.

Example #9:

Another lady was experiencing a three-year loan modification on her home, with frustrating attempts from the mortgage company. In desperation, she planted a seed believing God that he was going to do something. The Lord turned a frustrating situation into victory. The mortgage company re-modified her home and reduced the principle on her mortgage and lowered her payment. Who can do that but God? You can't pay for a miracle, but you can sow a seed believing that the power of God will step in giving glory unto no man but himself. You see, it's not in the amount that you sow— unless the Holy Spirit directs you to sow a specific amount—but it's out of obedience. As the Zarepheth woman experienced an incredible harvest, you will too as you plant this seed. You will experience a harvest in that area of your need.

Now, as you stand in faith believing in the grace of God to do the impossible in your life, when it comes embrace it with great joy and appreciation. For it was God who opened that door for you. Don't become an inspector of Gods grace? Let me explain

There's a familiar story in the parable that Jesus spoke of in Matthew 20:3-11, in which he talks about an estate owner hiring workers for his vineyard. He finds the workers and agrees on a certain wage of 1 penny a day and the workers began to work. As time progressed he came across more workers and hired them as well. This time he told the workers to start working and he will give them what is just and fair.

When evening had come the owner summoned for all the workers to come and he gave the workers that started later on in the day the same pay of 1 penny. That was grace! However, the workers that began their shift earlier didn't seem to think that, they began to analyze the rationale of how they qualified for the same pay.

When God blesses you receive it with joy, don't try to compare your blessing with those around you, because it took a miracle for you to receive what God gave you. I love what Jesus says in verse 16, he says "so the last shall be first and the first shall be last." Wow so don't get distracted with what's on around you, but rejoice in what God's getting ready to do in your life, because he is getting ready to great things. So wait in great expectancy.

Prayer

Father, thank you for this life-transforming season for my brother/sister. Thank you for restoration, health, wholeness, and increase in their life. Father, as they pray, they welcome you to step into their situation. We thank you for a sudden transformation in their life. Bless the seed they are sowing. Let it multiply 30, 60, and 100-fold according to your word to create a harvest in that area of their life. Take absolute control.

In Jesus Name, Amen!

Journal

Bibles References

Amplified (AMP)

English Standard Version (ESV)

King James Version (KJV)

New American Standard Bible (NASB)

New International Version (NIV)

New Literal Translation (NLT)

www.ingramcontent.com/pod-product-compliance
Lightning Source LLC
Chambersburg PA
CBHW060358050426
42449CB00009B/1786